Climacteric
Jo Bratten

First published 16th September 2022 by Fly on the Wall Press
Published in the UK by
Fly on the Wall Press
56 High Lea Rd
New Mills
Derbyshire
SK22 3DP

www.flyonthewallpress.co.uk
ISBN:9781913211844

A CIP Catalogue record for this book is available from the British Library.

For my sister, who knows it all already.

Contents

New Year's Day

Morning of the new year and I'm scrubbing
the bath, tugging snakes of hair
from the stinking drain, wondering
how so much of me got down here.

In the cold estuary I'm circling
black terns under a groggy sky,
tangling with pintails, shored on a tide
of mud with the plover and the lapwing,
stuck in the gullet of the godwit
and the rare avocet.
                                        I'm far out at sea
brining with molluscs, latching on
to cephalopods like flame, waking
somewhere in the belly of a whale,
retched up on your shore, a warning.

On Flood Street

Turne Erth to Water, and Water into Wynde,
Therof make Fire, and beware of the Floode

George Ripley

I've licked enough boots in this city to know
its streets are paved with blood, not gold; its silk

purses stitched from dead sows' ears, silver
spoons throttled from throats of tired mules;

gilded prayers leap from lepers' sores
while asses in high places snuff up air

like dragons; they've bought the city's silence,
flayed our ears, set our children's teeth on edge.

Consider the fire in the rivers, the swollen
fields, venom in the skies, blood in hedges;

consider the seething pot, the stock and stone;
consider the blackness of the toad, entombed

in the alchemist's vessel, a putrescent Christ
pierced through every side with colours rare.

Serious Verse

And do you write serious verse, he asks
as sweat gammons the tip

of his nose and today even the river
is thirsty, panting under the bridge

with the dried-up swans, and I think
I'd like to take it out for a drink,

slip my fingers into the crook of its arm,
lead it downstairs beyond the World's End

where I know this little cool place—
the kind that doesn't ask questions.

I'll buy it a dirty martini, extra olives,
no twist—*see, I know what you like.*

The river drinks like a navvy,
catching the oily pits in its teeth

before it spits them onto the floor,
flips off the bar where the men watch

appreciatively. Three drinks later
and the river's mine, all mine, sweetness

and brine and drunken pennywort; sighs gull
the hot night and it wants to come

home with me, lie down in front of the fan
and flood

In the shower with Gerard Manley Hopkins

Bless me father for I have sinned again
Rejoice for soapy foam-fleece fountain furled
For I have lied and cursed and fucked with men
Flashing quenching sing-shower curtain-curled
In hurting self and friend have careless been
Water of world of self-dew flesh-dew whirled
I wish to be blessed with some peace amen
With shower shining all sin stanched and swirled

Teach me the secrets of your skin so fine
Fresh-fire flashes fling off face soft and sing
The healing balms that help the hair to shine
Thirst quails parches quelled in the steam-sweet spring
I'll wash your bruisèd back if you wash mine
Wet wind-washed lovescape manshape rinse and wring

This is not a ~~love poem~~ poem about the moon

There's a witch living inside my mouth, bitch
to the last she makes freakish demands, shrieks
at night when I'm too tired to feed her, to spite me
gets in the way of my words, goes on hunger strikes
so I have to find her things I know she likes—
fingers, toads, fillets of snake, that sort of thing.
Sometimes I make her jellies in the shape of a cat
and when I'm in bed with a man she's there too,
clamping her jaws, not letting go, rushing into the street
with blood on her face, howling at children and dogs.
I'm not sure if I'm her familiar or she's mine.

Sometimes I lure her out from her bed behind
my lower left molar, stroke her belly, feed her
small slices of plum, eggy bread. Sorry, she says
but I want it to just be we two and rubs her pointy
head against my cheek. She makes me go outside
in the frost-studded night to look at the moon:
write me a moon poem, she says, sinking her teeth
into my arm and when I tell her it's a tired trope
she wrestles my pen, spits ink in my face, forces
my hand: write, she says, write something for me.

Because we have forgotten how to sleep

we are whispering our reasons to strangers;
we are googling our exes and symptoms:
there is a pain in a place; our legs all

electrical filaments, twanging; our hair
is coming out in clumps; we are sweeping
it from corners, from beneath the bed,

gathering it into our sleepless nest,
tumours hatching on our ribs like eggs;
our mouths are bubbling with hope

and peril; we are thinking up good titles
for poems; in the between spaces we are
having vivid dreams; mine are subaquatic:

I am dreaming of SpongeBob in a porno
with an octopus; they are touching
each other like rain; her tentacles slip-

pering through the yellow spaces of his flesh,
she is shimmering like caviar, all lips:
you are thinking there is a tenderness

in how her suckers clasp his little shorts;
you know it is not real but after all
these curdled nights you think it looks like love.

Rubbish Day

On Tuesday nights I double-bag the rubbish,
tightly wrap the bones and fat in rags, tuck
them in deep so the rats can't smell them;

tie the tops in triple-knots. The bags go
out before dawn and all Wednesday long
I wonder if my nasty little secrets are strewn

along the street. The rats have rooted out
the shame of others: the unwashed yoghurt pots,
browned avocado halves, unopened bags

of rotting fruit; I step over the wadded
tissues, the blackened tampon dredged
in coffee grounds; step around night sweats, break

ups, impotence, casual ingratitude, shattered
faith, final demands for payment. I'm rounding
the corner home, praying my pavement's clean.

I am drinking too much again

the river after sudden rain
    sap of pugnacious lilacs
the wild broth of a storm the cool
    air
between buildings   the late quartets
    audacious sunsets
    nightcaps of foxes and badgers and owls

find me at midnight face down by the pond
gulping up mud and glistening frogspawn
licking up slick ghosts in grass

so thirsty   I suck my smooth bones
            the sweet sharp marrow

    drinking my ice-cold sins like gin
    the little tin cans clink in the bin

Formication

Thou hast committed—
Fornication: but that was in another country;
And besides, the wench is dead. *Christopher Marlowe*

Small rooms lean in like confessionals
to take blood while we chant our latest plaints:
pains in the limbs, formication, lassitude.

Nurses in stout priest shoes tell us about their daughters
who study in Barcelona or Krakow; we too have been
there, arching our backs beneath foreign bridges,

under the fornicated arches of God's foreign houses,
in vaulted railway tavernas, deep in cold catacombs
among the grinning bones we have bent and cried.

Nurses who sighed like disappointed mothers
when we asked again for Levonelle (twice in two
months) pat our arms, ask us to place our fingers

on the cotton swab before they tape it down
and it is sweet relief when the ants finally appear,
having swarmed so long beneath the skin

it is joy to see them with their glossy purpose
pouring out like night beneath the whiteness
of the swab, seething queenward, a hot nuptial

flight spilling along our wrists, rising over
the nurses' needles and trays, filling the air
of the small room with blood and wings and sex.

Fall

Somewhere away from here apples are
thomping gladly to the ground,
giving their ripe bodies to the earth;

others stretching to keep stem and branch
together, unready for the fall, the damping
down of things, the slow oozings,

slower withering of leaf and seed,
the general slump of skin, flesh and core,
the happy clomping of the cider press

or rasp of rapacious wasp or winding
blindworm wrapping its gelatinous
body round and round, dreaming

it's a snake seeking a woman
to impress, undress, feed with apples
under a cold shrinking moon.

Dangerous Bodies

In the hospital we are more than flesh
bound. In its dim rooms we are plucked and stripped,
gowned and ungowned—slick of cold gel,
screen's gentle blink.
                                        Grapes bloom in my womb,
scalloping gourds, scrolling vines, unsucked fruit.

My body is acres of wine.
                                              It shames me
twice monthly birthing blood, the dreck and draff.
So much waste, it says.

In the hospital women sit inside
their vengeful bodies and wait, watch as a gurney
rolls past, its patient chained on both sides
to following guards, clipped and cuffed, gowned
in dangerous flesh, bound by organs of rage,
wheeled into a narrow room, knees raised.

In which I consider the body as a loaf

Sunday morning suddenly and my hands
are my mother's, deep in bread—an ocean

cold between us but in this bowl we meet
and I feel what it is to be her: to hold back

salt till the yeast quickens, knead without
anger, patience in the proving; I know

what it is to rise too fast and fall in the heat,
how the crumb disappoints and sags.

At my back I feel the busy sharpness
of blades, the toaster's red blaze; I fear

the tightness of the rack; I long to lose
myself in butter. Across the wide bowl

forty somewhere years to the west of me
a girl's thin fingers sift flour like time.

Home

And then sometimes you remember home:
gravel roads and coal pits and stray dogs,
winters that arrive, stay, refuse to leave,
little snows that stiffen grass into grey stone.
In summers, though, the thrill of those
dead hot days skiving up spoilbanks,
iron red pools hiding invisible fish,
canyons of grass, bushes of rusting rose.

And then sometimes you remember them:
the horses, the tall boys in denim,
the girls who tell you your legs are too thin,
the men whose hands never mean harm,
the friend who hangs herself at the back of the barn,
the righteous ones, looking at love, calling it sin.

Reclaimed

In these forgotten coal towns dust
pleats the air
          uncomfortably
sometimes it weeps   tiny
messy tears

at midnight
          the terrible shrill of coyotes
                              keening
  plotting an unthinkable
revenge   beyond the borders
of roads and google maps

the horizon burns all night

below their feet acres of shale
crack
          money flows west
rust from taps in the crippled
houses   streams clench
                              leach   creep

the coyotes never sleep
          calling something home   some
   thing   fierce and clean
spirits in the trees
     in the hills
taking themselves back

Unclean Thoughts

In the dark square of the confessional
they say you can talk about anything
but you're nine and don't have sins.

God gleams faintly in the mullioned brass
coaxing little pink sins like rhubarb, forced
so rudely into candle dredged air.

At fifteen you must tell the old man
about your unclean thoughts. You want to say
there is dust everywhere because everything

is shedding itself. You want to say it hurts
how squirrels seem to spill themselves
onto the road like red velvet cake.

You want to say you worry about death,
about a moment of reanimation
just as the grave is being sealed.

You want to say you don't want to believe
in the resurrection of the body.
You want to say the streams are full of murder.

Father clicks behind the expectant grille;
you say sorry for unclean thoughts; you say
one Our Father, ten Hail Marys, a Glory Be.

Allegory with a Virgin

Dad prayed for miracles, all day sometimes
in his upper room amid the drying beans
he stockpiled for the apocalypse.
So when Tony got out of prison
and started seeing the Virgin Mary
we packed into the old Toyota
to see for ourselves if the sun would spin.
You can smell roses when she appears, they said.
Our rosary beads of crushed rose petals
from Fatima or some other place
where the Virgin appeared to children
(*please do not appear to me*) sweated.
Old ladies crossed themselves. She is here!
they cried. The icon in St Jude's started
weeping, the statue in Our Lady of Mercy.
Rosaries and crosses turned to gold.
She appeared in the muddy field,
with a healing stream. Bishops circled
like hungry lions. Polaroids were sold,
gallons of holy water. She appeared with her son.
Miracles! they cried. Eyes that were blind
opened. Tumours shrunk and vanished.
Tumours the size of grapefruits.
Of clementines. Of kiwi fruits and grapes.
Whole fruit salads of tumours vanished overnight.

Tony kept a house full of wives, stole
another man's wife, then his daughter.
The bishops and the Virgin skipped town.
The blind boy stayed blind. Tony committed
felony, theft, possession of marijuana, abduction,
bad checks, carrying concealed weapons,
probation violations and unlawful possession
of explosive materials. He stockpiled guns
and the FBI came to town, with gas masks
and bulletproof vests, stopped for snacks.
Did you ever see anything like it! they cried.
Never made sandwiches for the FBI,
said the woman at the filling station.
What kind of sandwiches, they asked?
Turkey, she said proudly, and American.

Chiaroscuro

In the fractured dark we're all doomscrolling
before dawn, lit up like Caravaggios:

arms stretched across burning beds,
brows trenched like Judith surveying the head

of Holofernes caught against her bright blade,
baffling our morning brains with fresh dread.

In the pale light of refrigerator dawn
we stroke our kettles, wake our computers,

watch the same horrors play on bigger screens.
Tag yourself: Salome looking away,

the dispassionate crone, the white-shouldered
executioner with pity in his lips,

the head of the prophet on the platter
lit like pearl, all played out, prophecies stopped.

Epicedium

In a room somewhere a woman chooses
the clothes to bury her husband in.

How small they seem huddled there in the box.
How hard it is not to turn and look back.

She knows she is good at loss: mother, son,
father, husband. Women are used to bleeding.

His pockets she fills with seeds: corn in one,
beans in the other. Scarabs unwinged.

Think of the beans settling into earth,
splitting like pupae, spitting out of the dark.

Underlying Heart Problems

It's the day of my father's funeral
(we have to stream it since we're a month
into the pandemic) and there must be something
wrong with my heart too
all I can think about is my pot of geraniums
how someone stole it from my window
while I slept
                how someone eyed its red bloom
thought I'll have that and the cheap pot it's in
and walked off into the jaundiced night.

I picture it now thirsting
in a weed-struck yard
on a balcony delighting
a row of empty mayonnaise jars
dropped on its side in the playground
by the supermarket
its heart of soil collapsing
into dark.

I file a police report [theft] [one plant]
interrogate the blackened spot
where it sat as if stained paint can explain
the thudding absence.

I should leave a note
please bring back my geraniums
please have mercy and don't take the others
please take them all if they bring you joy
in this piteous time
                        please send help
I'm over here drowning in metaphor.

Dear Heavenly Father

of course I pray but not in your way (yet
who more than you taught me to pray here
at the church of the sky, to kneel in dirt, bless

the gentle worms, millipedes, pill bugs, all
our friends in the soil) I tell my gratitude
like beads, tell it to the gold-husked bees

the dandelion weeds I leave to flower
for earth (father) for bread (mother)
for butter and salt (sister and brother)

prayer blossoms in my mouth like wine
holds up the day as a chalice blessed
fleshes hollow cells with pip and pith

you left your words in our hands to shell
shuck and gather so we unwrite/rewrite
how your prayers roused sleeping heaven

stirred seraph and trumpet, how you shouldered
off past the spitting waves and took flight
just as the world was beginning to end.

Distancing

Days standing at the edge of myself
hovering in the blurred bits
watching me stage this masque of brisk

efficiency—admiring my aplomb
grimacing at the cut of my jib
skulking past the corner of my eye.

Nothing to do with myself but walk
carry these shadow ends like foundlings
seek a street silent enough to hear

the squeak of my boots on scrubbed
pavement—that discomfiting trochaic
cadence—*it's me it's me it's me it's me.*

Searching for God in the Asda Carpark

We're gathered here this wet Sunday morning,
blossom on weeds like offerings of praise;

we pause in the aisles in search of redemption,
hymns sing from the tills as service begins.

Magpies in the muddy playground jab
at crisp packets shining below the swings:

at least they mourn their dead, she says,
the girl who looks for lost things. They make

wreaths of old grass and twigs like broken nests
for fallen friends. Sweetie, we've all been there,

you want to say, leaning on that railing
to steady your head, spotting the piece of yourself

you'd given away lying with cans
and cigarette ends. Lost gods haunt the car park

searching for those who'd loved them. I AM
sprayed on the brick like a burning bush.

In Gaza, bombs fall on an orange grove
and you hold your loss sticky in your birthless

hands. In the shelter of the covered walkway
a woman smiles and asks if I know what God is:

the lie like silver spills from my lips, spins in rings,
finds its way to the beggar's empty cup.

The traffic surges on the road behind—
somewhere, a bird cries and beats its wings.

Blackberries

August comes as it always does and with it
come the blackberries, tangling up hedgerows,
strangling children and glutting the thrushes.

And here they are on the A3205 between
a Halfords and a bus stop, blobbing darkly
amongst municipal lavender. Do I dare

place one on my tongue? Will it bleed
diesel? They survey me with suspicion;
no one has ever looked at them this hard.

It's not their flesh I want, their summer
sugared blood—all that bromidic communion.
Give me a perilous quest, a red thrust

into sticky biting thickets, the hunt
for the thing expected but still unfound,
just beyond that tree, behind that leaf—

that thing at the forest edge where the light
simpers like it knows you, like it knew how
you would shred yourself to bits to find you.

Solace

After such a summer you want to wield
words like scythes but only softness comes;
what needs such violence in the season

of plums: sloes wax blue through blackthorn,
fubsy bullaces bloom black and gold,
greengage, damson, mirabelle, merryweather,

Warwickshire droopers, Shropshire prunes,
all these kind bright drupes spooning in the sun—
see, the sound of soft fruits singing together.

Solstice

I don’t mind the dark so much going home
as the days tilt us further from the light;
the shiver of air crossing the river,
thunder from fog-plumed highways,
far off trains necklacing the night.

I miss cars in darkness seen from a plane,
reassuring red lights travelling towards
someone, little houses cradled in snow,
warm furniture, cats testing the edges
of themselves, waiting for you.

The grey plover is a delightful wader

I wish to winter alone
deep in the coastal marshes
sheltered
standing and watching
running forward
pecking
then standing still again

I wish to go grey in winter
call it
my non-breeding plumage
remain out of sight

we are not gregarious
fly up
when disturbed
flashing the blackness
under our wings

we dream sometimes
Veneto beaches
golden plovers who wade in flocks
stand in pairs
bask in sun

but we like the rain

to stand alone in the shallows
to wade
when the spring rains fall
delightfully

Scant Ground

He always asks me if I have a garden
(for on this ground only can we avoid
quarrel) and I again explain that space

in the city belongs to the rich, explain
student loans, mortgages, interest rates;
he asks me when I got to be so dumb,
explains again the economy of seeds.

I scan my little patch of ground, my bit
of earth. So bricked and gridded nothing will
grow. The cramped soil winces at my trowel

edge, peels like old lino, coughs its bones bare
and breathes a clean dirty smell to root in.
In this narrow plot I plant his words, pull weeds,
bless rain. His hand on my shoulder like air.

Crab in my hand

Crab in my hand   do you long
to ride the buttery wing of morning

glide slow across the face of day
shrug your cracked carapace away

feast on the brew of afternoon
catch eternity with your claws

hold it fast in your pleopods
watch it hatch into shining rings

clasp them round your dactyls
fix them to your pollex like stars

plate yourself in flashing armour
stride sideways in inviolable blue?

Crab in my hand   I do too.

Sunset Over Watford

I am not terribly good at love. Yet
I begin to think I could be if love
is loving small things: the moment when
the second magpie lurches across the path;
the girl in the purple coat running
towards the dog she doesn't know; old men
on the bench with sandwiches in the rain;
the back of your neck; breathing you in quick
thick gulps, like cold water after bedtime;
the smell of dying daffodils that still
strain to hold their heads towards
the February sun as it sets over
Uxbridge, Ruislip, Pinner, Hatch End, Watford—
all bright and glittering in the smoky air.

Notes on poems

'In the shower with Gerard Manley Hopkins' borrows liberally from Hopkins's verse. Hopkins's nickname at school was 'Skin' because his was so lovely.

'Formication' employs a pun, on the double meaning of 'fornicated', from John Milton's *The Reason of Church-Government Urg'd against Prelaty.*

'Reclaimed' alludes to the so-called reclamation of land that was formerly coal-mined.

'Allegory with a Virgin' is based on the story of a man in a small town in Ohio who convinced a lot of people (including my father) that the Virgin Mary was appearing to him. In other supposed apparitions, such as Fatima and Medjugorje, spectators reported that the sun would spin or there would be a smell of roses when the Virgin Mary appeared.

'The grey plover is a delightful wader' takes its title from the first line of the late Derwent May's 'Nature Notes' on the grey plover, published in the *Times.*

'Sunset Over Watford' is obviously indebted to Wordsworth for its final line.

Acknowledgements and thanks

Some of these poems were first published in *Ambit, Acumen, Butcher's Dog, Finished Creatures, Ink Sweat & Tears, One Hand Clapping, Poetry Birmingham, Poetry Bus, The North, The Rialto* and *Under the Radar*. 'Sunset Over Watford' is featured on *Iamb: Poetry Seen and Heard.*

I am endlessly grateful to the editors who read and liked these poems (and said nothing about the bad ones) and especially to Isabelle Kenyon; to Mark Antony Owen, Naush Sabah, Louise Peterkin, Luke Wright and others who have championed my writing; to my writing pals (Rebecca, Jonathan, Lauren, Zoë, Lucy) for reading poems in various incarnations and nodding improvingly; to my parents (on earth and in heaven), for teaching us to love words and plants and creatures.

Author Biography

Jo's poetry has been published in *Ambit, bath magg, Butcher's Dog, The Interpreter's House, The North, Poetry Birmingham Literary Journal, The Rialto* and *Under the Radar*, amongst others. Originally from the USA, Jo completed a PhD at the University of St Andrews and lives in London. Climacteric is her debut chapbook.

Fly on the Wall Press

A publisher with a conscience.
Publishing high quality anthologies, novels, short stories and poetry on pressing issues, from exceptional writers around the globe. Founded in 2018 by founding editor, Isabelle Kenyon.

Some other publications:

The Woman With An Owl Tattoo by Anne Walsh Donnelly

the sea refuses no river by Bethany Rivers

The Prettyboys of Gangster Town by Martin Grey

The Sound of the Earth Singing to Herself by Ricky Ray

Inherent by Lucia Orellana Damacela

Medusa Retold by Sarah Wallis

Pigskin by David Hartley

We Are All Somebody

Aftereffects by Jiye Lee

Someone Is Missing Me by Tina Tamsho-Thomas

*Odd as F*ck by Anne Walsh Donnelly*

Muscle and Mouth by Louise Finnigan

Modern Medicine by Lucy Hurst

These Mothers of Gods by Rachel Bower

Sin Is Due To Open In A Room Above Kitty's by Morag Anderson

Fauna by David Hartley

How To Bring Him Back by Clare HM

No One Has Any Intention of Building A Wall by Ruth Brandt

Warriors by Sundra Lawrence

Social Media:

@fly_press (Twitter) @flyonthewall_poetry (Instagram)

@flyonthewallpress (Facebook) www.flyonthewallpress.co.uk